MY FRIEND JOHN

By Pete DeWorken

Cover Design by Pete DeWorken

Book Design by Lorie DeWorken, MindtheMargins.com

Photos by Pete DeWorken, Samantha Murray

ISBN: 0615537952

ISBN-13: 978-0615537955

DEDICATION

To my wife,
the only person who's taken more crap from me than John.

ACKNOWLEDGEMENTS

Thanks to all my friends and family who made this dirty little book possible:

God...because I'm going to hell if I don't start with him. Put no other God before Him...including the porcelain ones.

Then a close second, but only by a smidgen, my wonderful wife for her encouragement, patience, and warped sense of humor that made this book sound like a good idea.

My friend Steve-O who's potty mouth and sick bathroom jokes set the wheels in motion for this book.

Those who did the back-breaking work of helping me lug this toilet around for pictures - Sam Murray, Aaron Roy, Brian Sparks, and my eldest beauty, Bonnie DeWorken.

Wells Fargo for kicking me out of my house and giving me the reason to write about My Friend John.

Fljer for manufacturing a sweet little piece of plumbing for pleasurable posterior placement - a shout out to Marc Leslie.

The City of Galveston, TX for the quirky and wide ranging scenery to photograph My Friend John.

Mom for not thinking I'm an idiot for writing this...at least not saying it out loud.

Dad for passing down your horrible digestive issues to me, thus giving me the much needed time to ponder bathroom humor...while in the bathroom.

My friends who let me test out the content and humored me even when the jokes didn't humor them.

INTRODUCTION

In May 2011, the culmination of my family's financial struggles came to a head when we lost our home to foreclosure. It was a difficult time to say the least—accepting the loss, packing up our belongings, and simply saying goodbye to everything in our home...except for one thing. The one thing we could not say goodbye to... My Friend, John.

John is a commode I gleaned from a construction project I managed years prior, and he is no ordinary toilet. He's an old-school, full flush, non-eco-friendly, H_2O guzzler. He would have been perfect for the basement bathroom project we had dreamed of that never came to fruition.

Although we never got to build that bathroom, our dreams of using John one day did not fade away. So we made a crazy decision and loaded John on the back of our family van, along with the last of our belongings, and we hit the road.

This book is a tribute to My Friend John, and all that could have been if I had ever gotten to install him in our bathroom-to-be. This is also a reflection on the relationship I've had with one of the most common, unappreciated, and unsung heroes of all our lives. This book sheds light on the many aspects of a life-long love for this porcelain god.

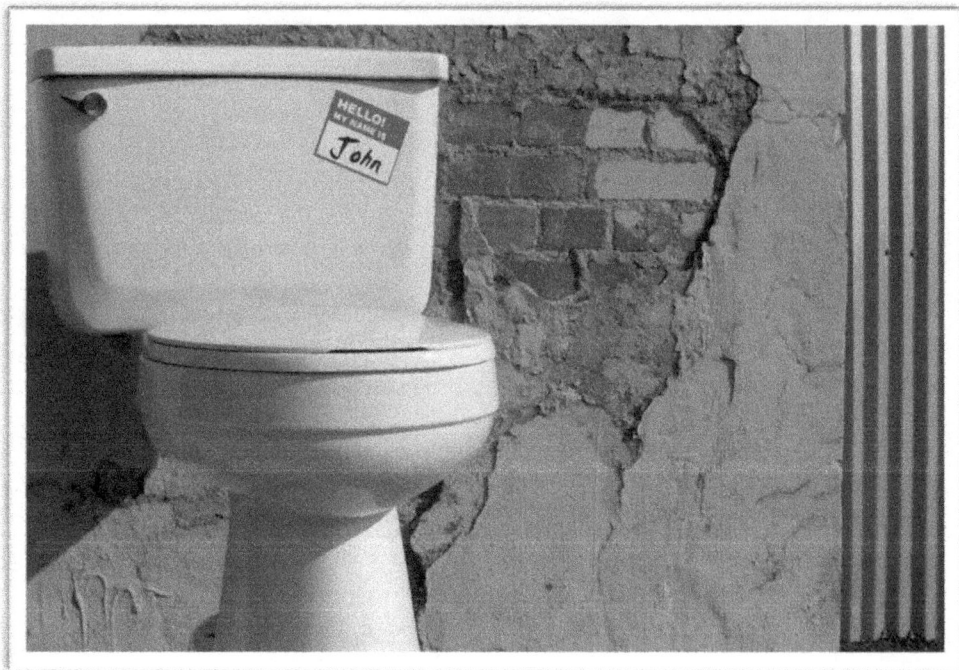

John has never seen my good side.

MY FRIEND JOHN

After what I just did to him,
John might just file for aggravated assault.

John's got a big mouth.

MY FRIEND JOHN

John felt like I really unloaded on him today.

My friend John is full of **it.

**MY FRIEND
JOHN**

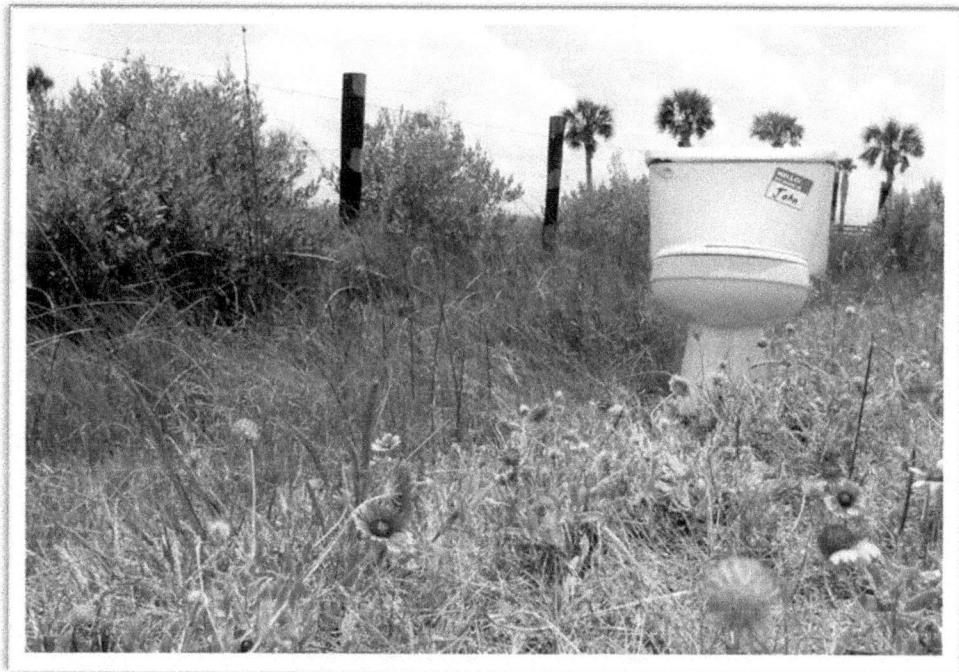

John just sits there and takes it all in.

MY FRIEND JOHN

John really takes a lot of crap from me...
and he doesn't complain.

John hates asparagus.

MY FRIEND
JOHN

John's coming down with something...
he's pretty stopped up this morning.

I feel like I can really let go when I'm with John.

MY FRIEND JOHN

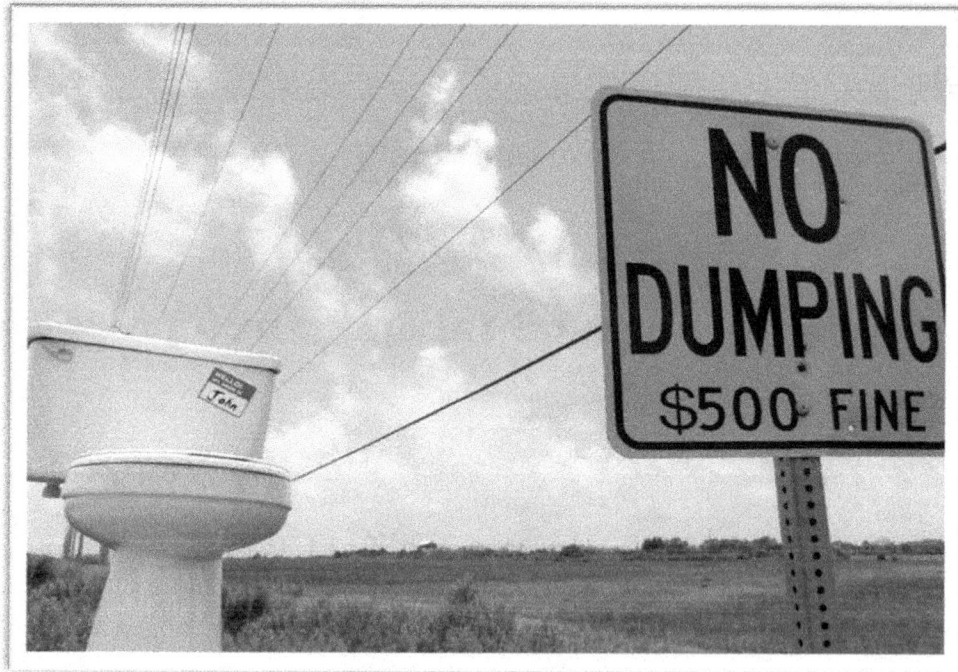

John thinks I'm a big ass.

MY FRIEND JOHN

**John is as uncomfortable
with feminine products as I am.**

John always listens when I ass him a question.

MY FRIEND
JOHN

John can see right into me.

John understands when I have to run.

MY FRIEND JOHN

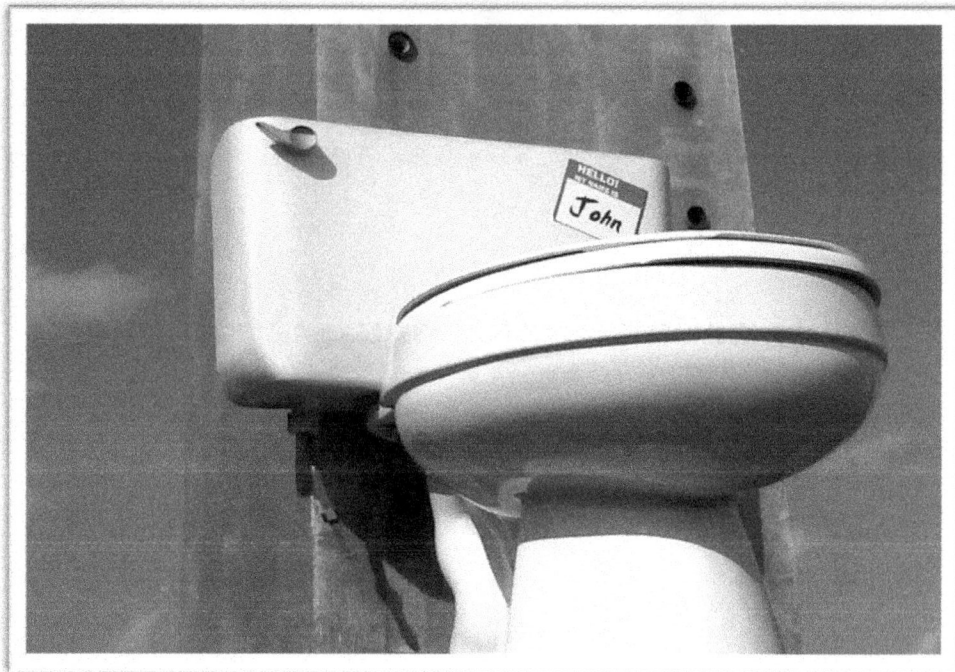

John has always been a great support.

**MY FRIEND
JOHN**

John thinks I'm a bit of a drip.

John is happy to help when
I have a load to drop at the dump.

**MY FRIEND
JOHN**

John knows when I should be trying harder.

John has seen me
when I have pushed myself too far.

**MY FRIEND
JOHN**

John has a blast when we're together.

**MY FRIEND
JOHN**

John doesn't handle big gifts very well.

John never forgets to leave water out for my dog.

MY FRIEND JOHN

John doesn't think I'm anal retentive.

I just had a long sit-down with John.

**MY FRIEND
JOHN**

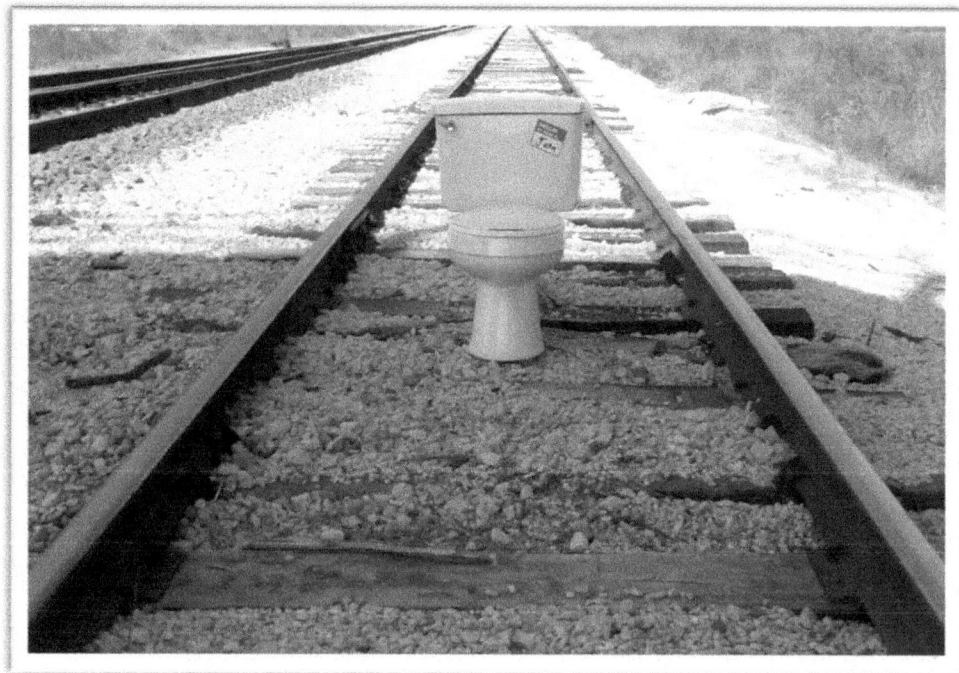

John is one cool dude.

MY FRIEND
JOHN

John won't come out of his room.

John can't keep his mouth shut.

MY FRIEND JOHN

Before I even got started with John,
he flipped his lid.

John has a filthy mouth.

MY FRIEND JOHN

36

John is my business partner.

**MY FRIEND
JOHN**

**John doesn't laugh when I drop my pants...
even when it's cold.**

I just laid a big one on my friend John.

**MY FRIEND
JOHN**

**John knows how to handle himself
when I dump on him.**

John is always up for a sit-in.

MY FRIEND JOHN

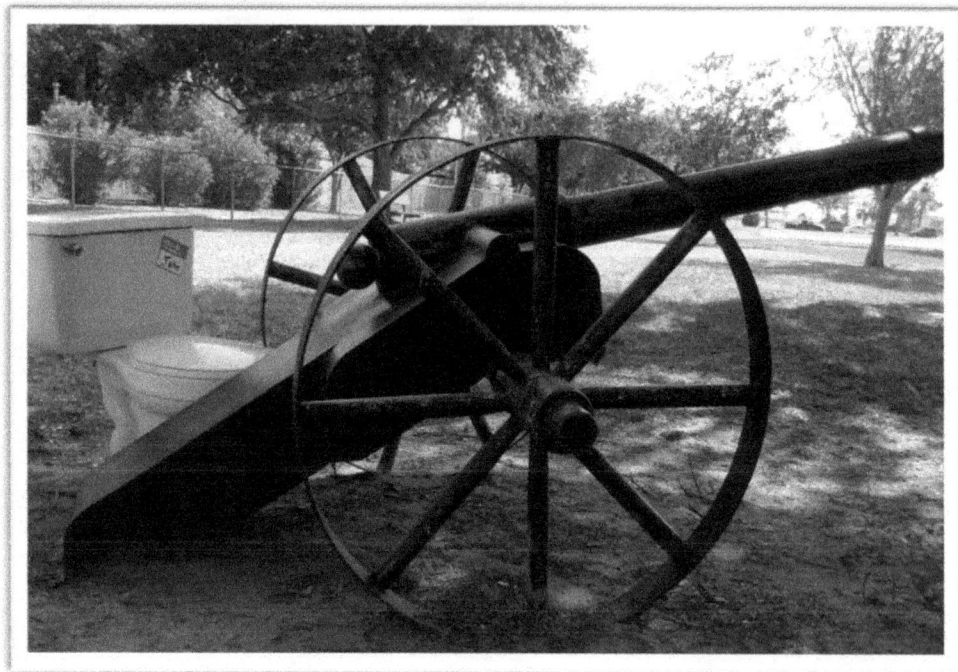

John doesn't say a word...
even when he knows I'm about to blow it.

MY FRIEND JOHN

Whenever I'm around,
John goes to a dark, dark place.

John doesn't budge, even when I fart in his face.

MY FRIEND
JOHN

Every time I'm with John I just feel moved.

John's a not-so-tall drink of water.

**MY FRIEND
JOHN**

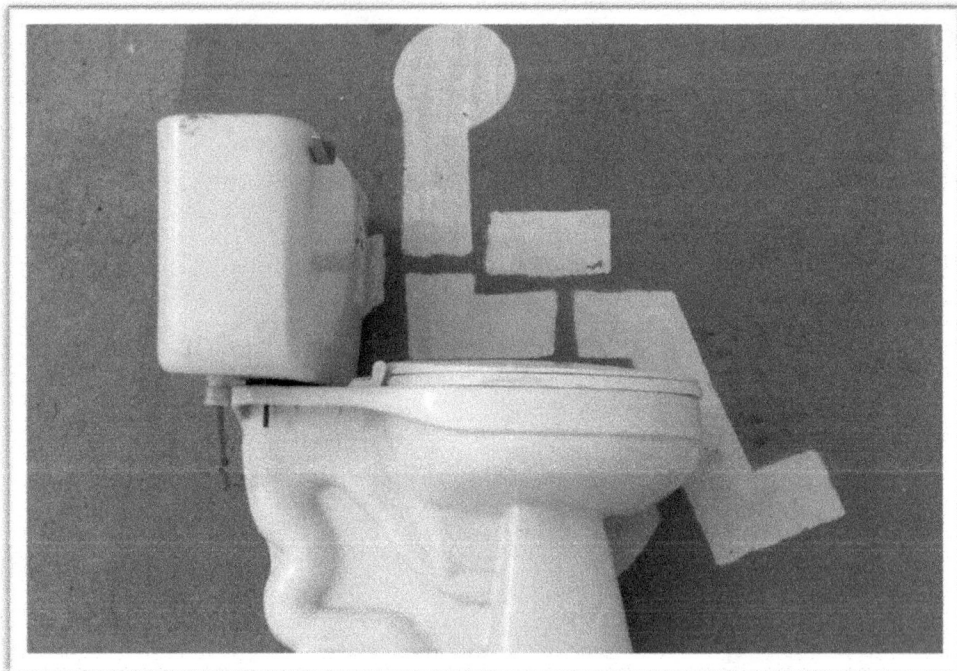

When I'm with John, he just puts me at ease.

MY FRIEND JOHN

John looks a little blue today.

John really puts me on a pedestal.

**MY FRIEND
JOHN**

I really dropped a bomb on John today.

John will let me unload on him
at a moment's notice.

**MY FRIEND
JOHN**

John hates to see me leave,
but loves to watch me go.

MY FRIEND JOHN

John doesn't like chairs, he prefers stools.

John really knows how to carry a load.

MY FRIEND JOHN

John's favorite planet is Uranus.

It's a mystery to me
why John gets so choked up sometimes.

MY FRIEND JOHN

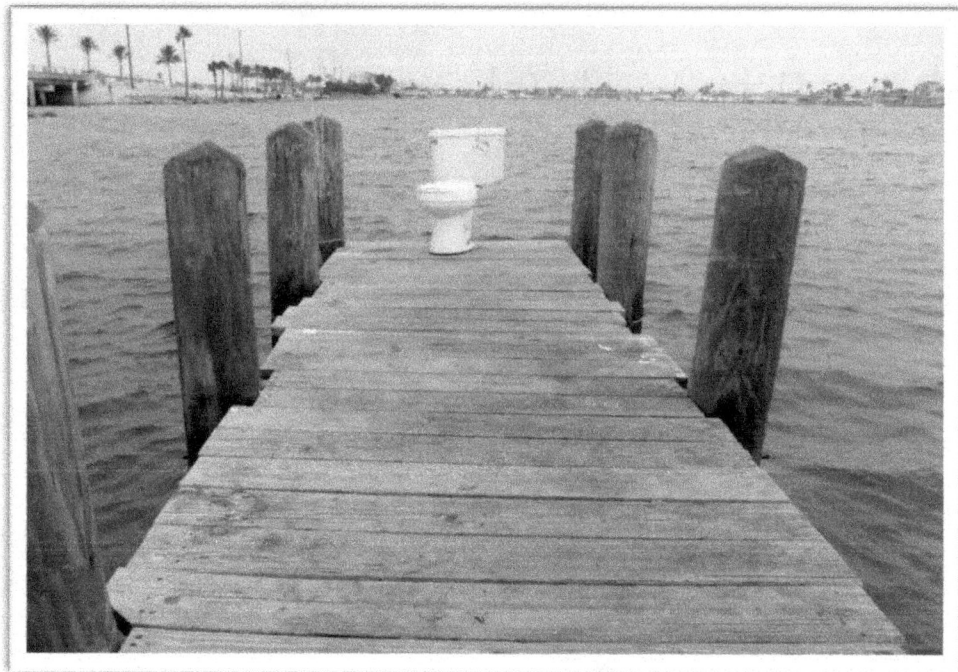

John really knows how to float my boat.

MY FRIEND
JOHN

John saw me coming and just thought, "Oh, sh**."

My friend John is loaded.

MY FRIEND JOHN

John's always willing to handle my extra paperwork.

John watches what I eat.

**MY FRIEND
JOHN**

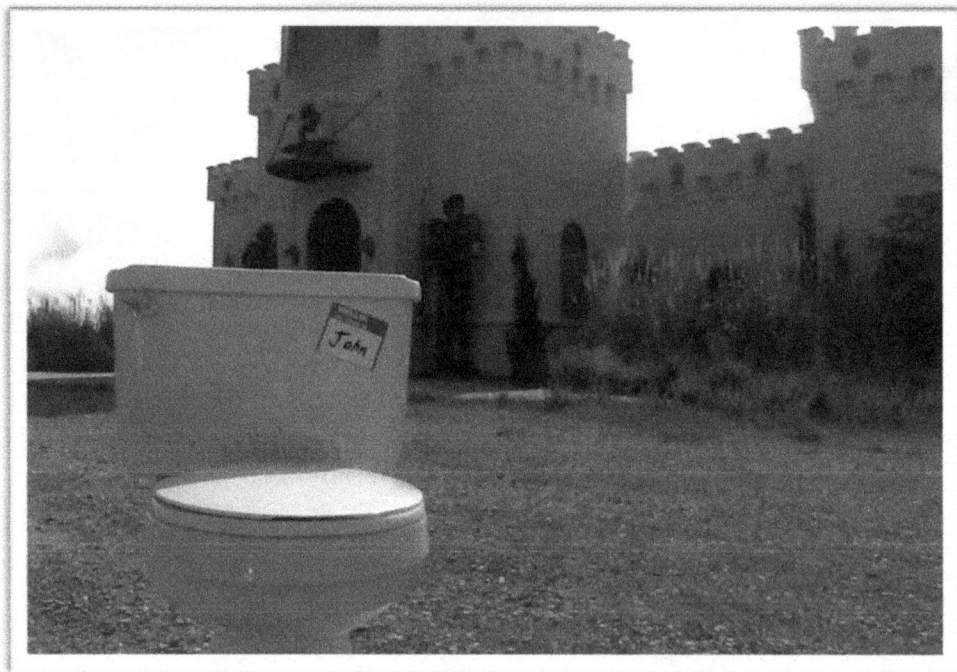

John was holding a royal flush.

**MY FRIEND
JOHN**

I take time to share something with John every day.

When John is overwhelmed, he just starts gushing.

MY FRIEND JOHN

John just came in turd place.

**The secret to my relationship with John
is that we're willing to stay open with each other.**

**MY FRIEND
JOHN**

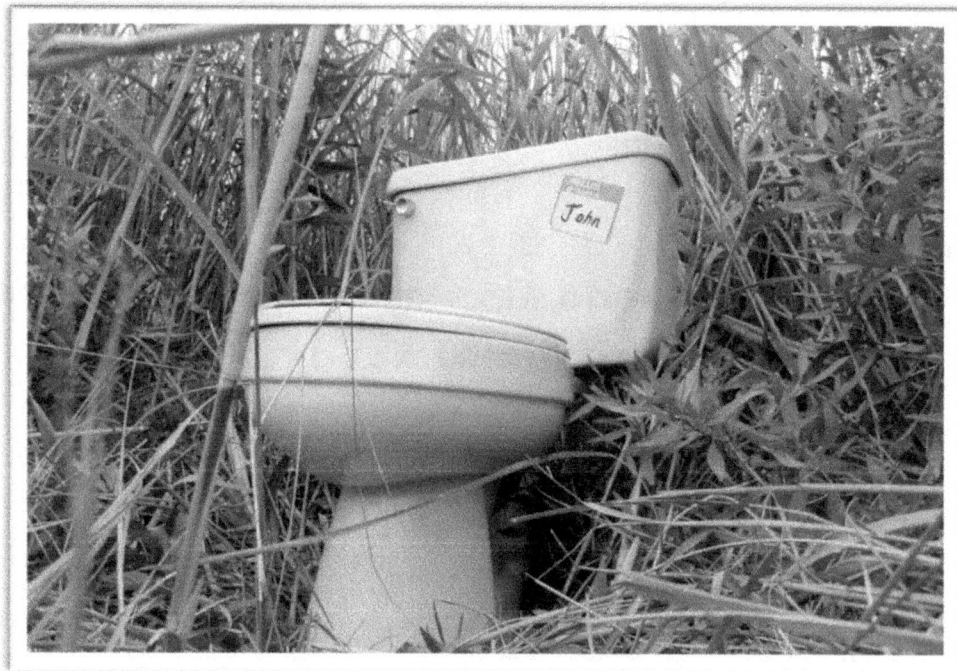

John says deuces are wild.

MY FRIEND
JOHN

John was willing to open up to me
the first time we met.

I think I just killed John.

**MY FRIEND
JOHN**

John loves watching shuttle launches.

When I just can't keep it to myself,
I know I can share it with John.

MY FRIEND JOHN

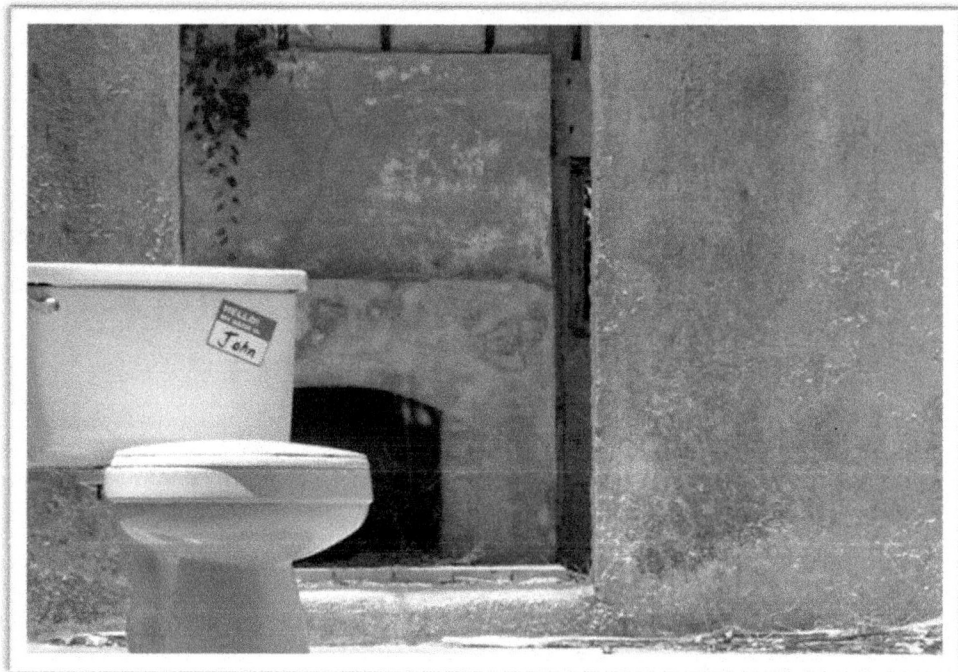

John should be a mason.
He's great at helping me lay bricks.

MY FRIEND JOHN

I had to help John get out of a jam.

I had a special delivery for John today.

MY FRIEND JOHN

John knows my secret log-in.

John is really well-connected.

MY FRIEND
JOHN

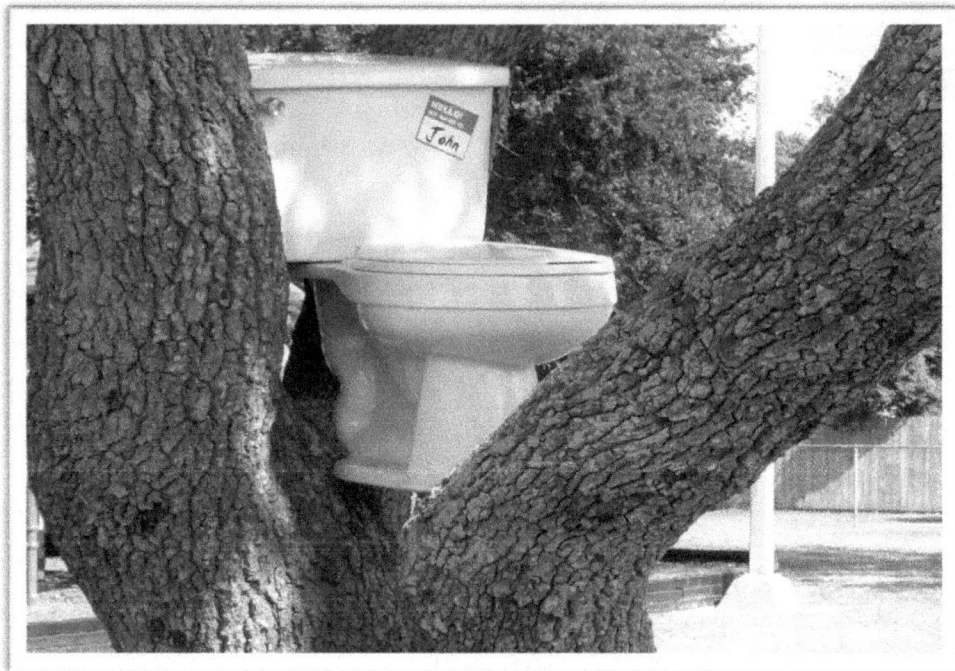

John loves to watch me work.

MY FRIEND JOHN

John knows each entry in my captain's log.

John thinks I'm a great bowler.

**MY FRIEND
JOHN**

**John couldn't believe
I was carrying so much baggage.**

John and I played craps all night.

**MY FRIEND
JOHN**

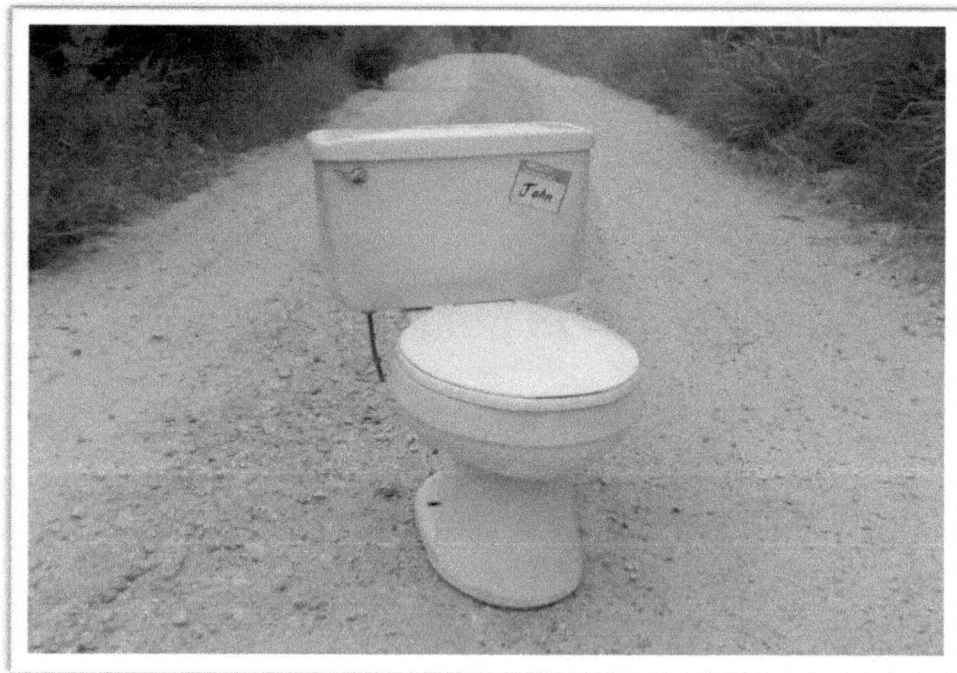

John likes to take me on my runs.

**MY FRIEND
JOHN**

John thinks I give the best gifts.

John hates it when I'm all sappy.

**MY FRIEND
JOHN**

**When I'm feeling sick,
I just can't bring myself to let go of John.**

John likes to call me Squirt.

**MY FRIEND
JOHN**

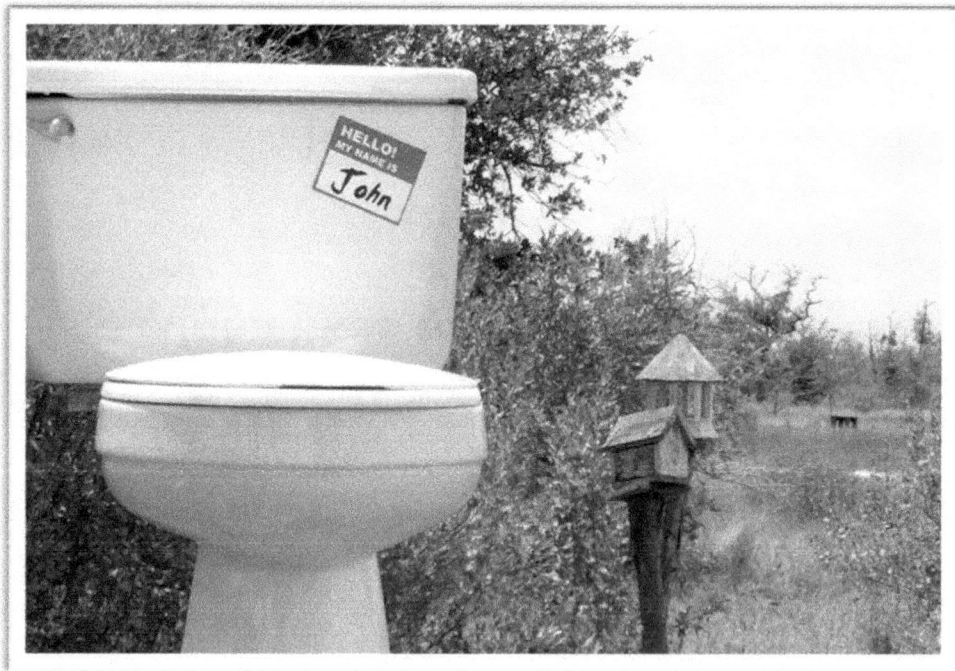

John can't wait 'til I stock the pond.

MY FRIEND JOHN

I'm pretty sure John is being abused at home.

I never have to tell John when I have to go.

**MY FRIEND
JOHN**

John knows I'm a real solid guy.

John knows it's the bowl game that really matters.

MY FRIEND
JOHN

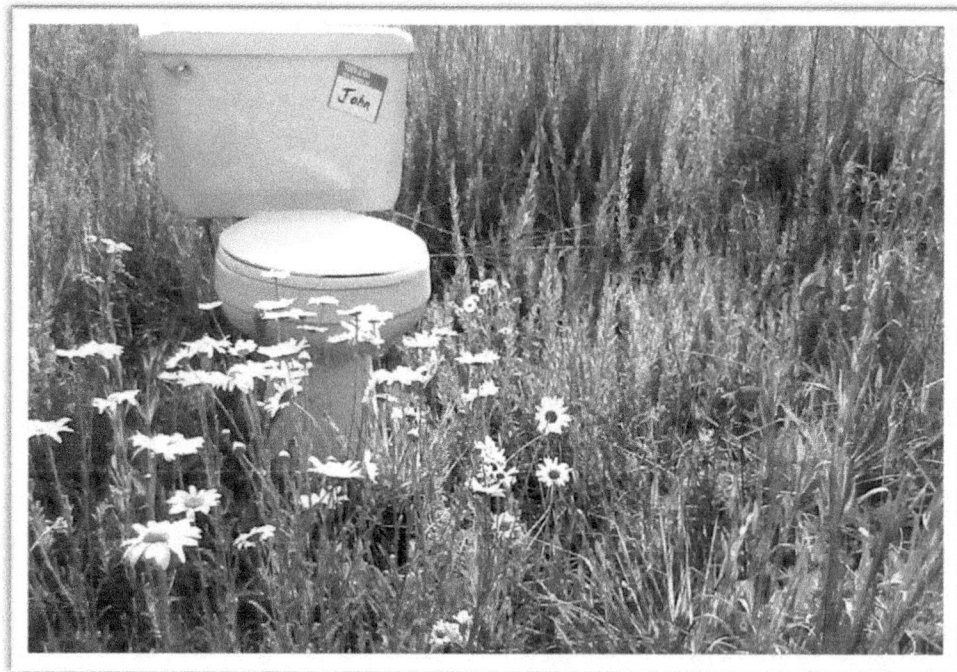

John thinks I'm a nice shot.

**MY FRIEND
JOHN**

John is an avid cigar collector.

I left John void of any substance.

MY FRIEND JOHN

I just went off on John, and he didn't deserve it.

John considers me a real whiz kid.

MY FRIEND JOHN

John thinks I can make a real splash.

**MY FRIEND
JOHN**

John doesn't mind if I just piddle around.

John can really take some punishment.

MY FRIEND JOHN

John thinks I'm a real paper pusher.

John never tells me to get off my butt.

MY FRIEND JOHN

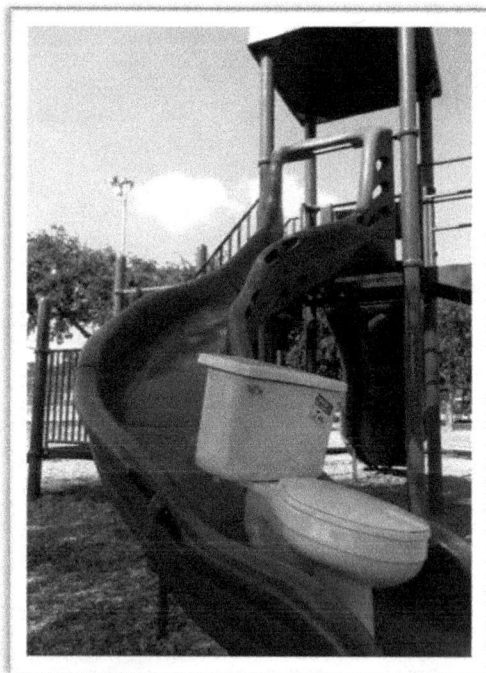

John knows I actually ache for him in the morning.

**MY FRIEND
JOHN**

John and Willy are on a first name basis.

John thinks I just blew him a kiss.

MY FRIEND JOHN

John just got tanked.

John always tunes in for the explosive finale.

MY FRIEND
JOHN

John's a crack addict.

**MY FRIEND
JOHN**

I don't think John is going to
get over that for a while.

John thinks my privates are first-class.

MY FRIEND JOHN

I took John to a blowout sale today.

John knows when I'm wiped.

MY FRIEND
JOHN

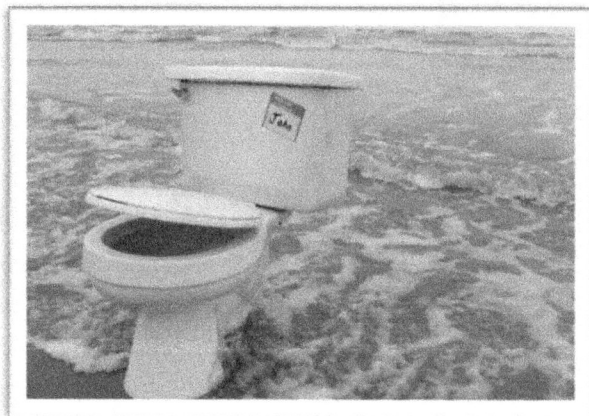

John lives like it's a full moon every night.

MY FRIEND JOHN

I ripped John a new one.

John knows I really only stand for one thing.

**MY FRIEND
JOHN**

John likes it when I toot my own horn.

After what I just did to John,
I may have reversed his circulation.

MY FRIEND
JOHN

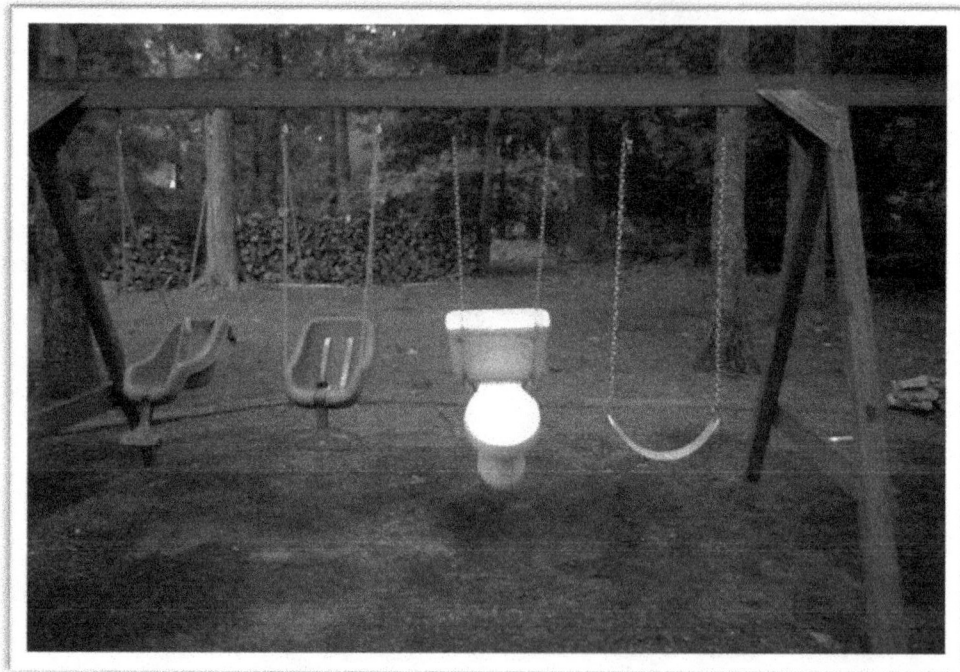

John won't let me flush my future down the drain, but he sure knows how to help me let go of my past.

MY FRIEND JOHN

I really laid into John last night.

I poured everything I had into John.

MY FRIEND JOHN

John thinks my fart jokes are hilarious.

John isn't ever going to change his mind.
He really only has one point of view.

**MY FRIEND
JOHN**

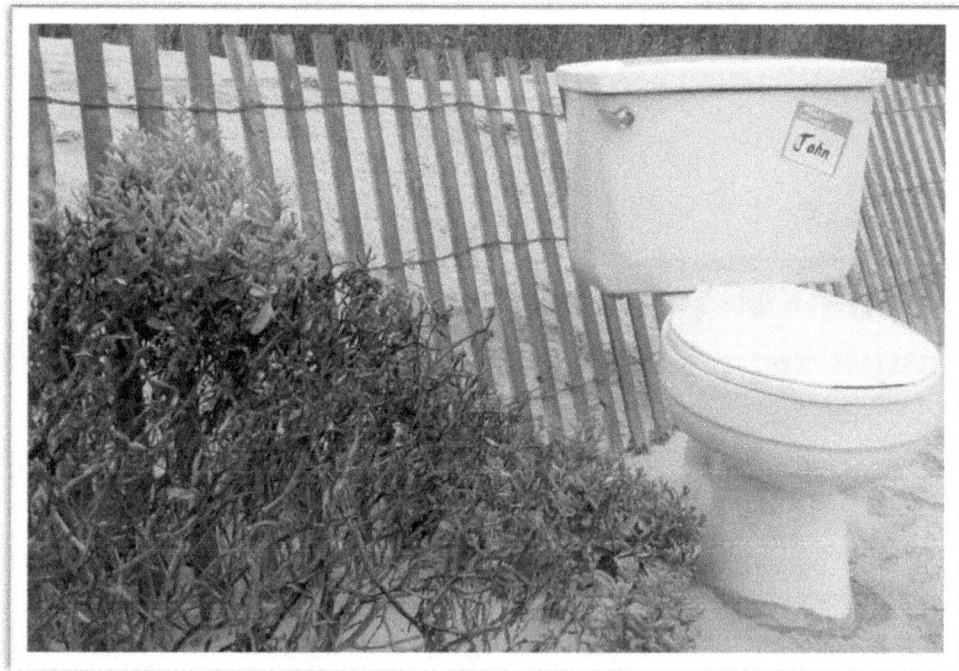

**John has witnessed
many senseless acts of violence.**

**MY FRIEND
JOHN**

John really mixes things up.

John never takes another call
when we're in a meeting.

MY FRIEND
JOHN

I hate seeing John out in public.

At least with John,
you know the sh** will never hit the fan.

MY FRIEND
JOHN

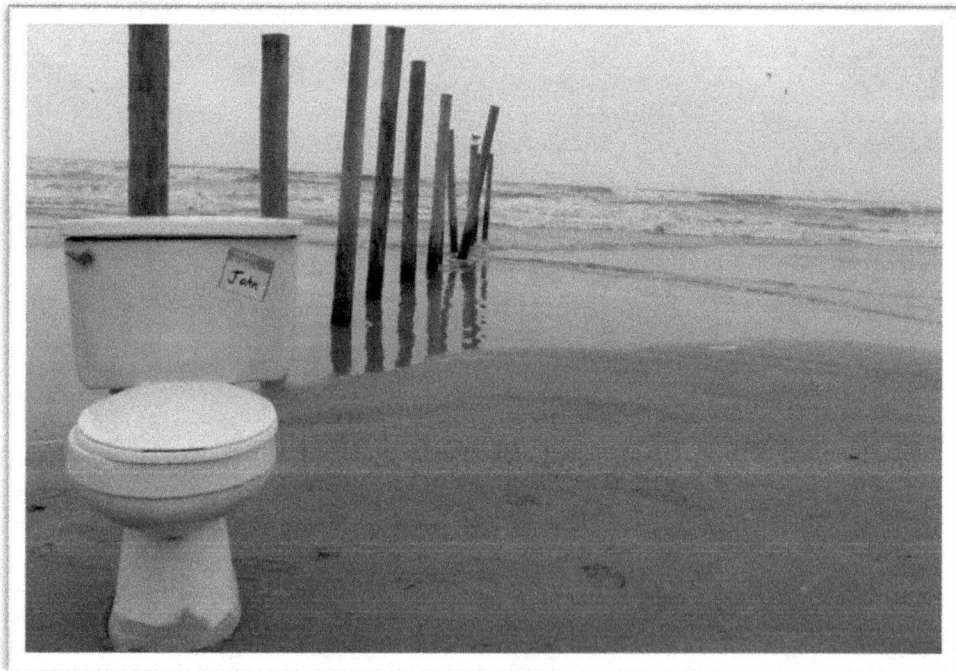

John loves it when you settle down
and share your tail with him.

MY FRIEND
JOHN

I've never seen John come unhinged.

John sticks around, even when things get messy.

MY FRIEND JOHN

It's a good thing John doesn't drive.
The number of times he's been
rear-ended is astonishing.

John has a great set of pipes.

**MY FRIEND
JOHN**

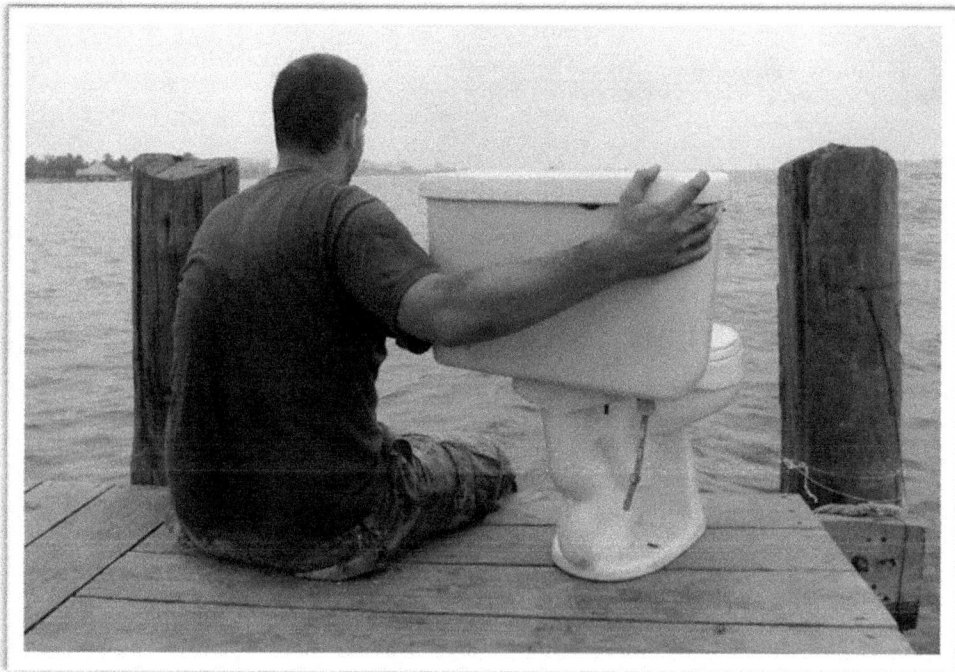

ABOUT THE AUTHOR

Pete DeWorken is a husband, father to 3 amazing daughters, and former bad-tempered, foul-mouthed contractor from Virginia who now runs a disaster relief ministry.

This is his first bathroom humor book.

Follow Pete on Twitter (@TheBSMissionary)
and follow John on Twitter (@My_Friend_John)!

**MY FRIEND
JOHN**

To share your own reflections
on the relationship we've all had with
one of the most common, unappreciated, and
unsung heroes of all time --

Go to **www.MyFriendJohn.com** TODAY!

Follow John on Twitter (@My_Friend_John)!

**MY FRIEND
JOHN**